PELE B

THE LIFE OF STRUGGLE AND

TRIUMPH OF PELE

JOHNSON TITUS

CHAPTER ONE

PELE'S EARLY YEARS

Nicknamed Pele was born On October 23, 1940, in Três Coraçes, Minas Gerais, Brazil. His full name was Edson Arantes do Nascimento. Pele, who is the eldest of three children grew up in the underprivileged area of Três Coraçes. He started practising soccer and soon established himself as a skilled player. He was asked to join the club's youth system at 15 after being discovered by a scout from Santos FC, a professional soccer team in Brazil. Pelé moved to Santos to enrol in the school, where he rapidly established a reputation as a quality young player. In 1956, he made his Santos professional debut and rapidly established himself as an essential member of the squad. Pelé stood out thanks to his talent, speed, and scoring prowess, and he rose to the position of a star player for Santos. He scored more than 1,000 goals for the club and contributed to the squad winning several national and international championships. Pelé's career was launched by his triumph with Santos.

Pelé played for Brazil's national squad in addition to his club career. He made his international debut in 1957, participated in four World Cups, and helped Brazil win the competition in 1958, 1962, and 1970. In the 1958 and 1970 World Cups, Pelé led the competition in goals scored and was crowned the best player in both years. In 92 games for the Brazilian national team, he scored 77 goals scored. Pelé started working in a number of businesses after he stopped playing soccer, including coaching and team ownership. He also participated in several humanitarian endeavours and served as a television pundit and business spokesman. Also being inducted into the International and Brazilian Football Halls of Fame, Time magazine named Pelé one of the 100 most important persons in the world in 2004. Numerous achievements and milestones during Pelé's career served as markers. He is the top scorer for Santos FC and the Brazilian national team. The only pele who amassed over 1,000 goals in his professional career. He was awarded the World Cup's best player thrice and won three World Cup championships with Brazil. In addition to his World Cup victories, Pelé also won multiple local championships with Santos FC, including the Brazilian league title and the Copa Libertadores, South America's top club tournament. During his playing career, Pelé was regarded as the finest player in the world because of his talent, pace, and scoring prowess. He was noted for his ability to score amazing goals and was also a superb facilitator and finisher. Pelé was a versatile player who could play as a striker or an offensive midfielder. He was equally skilled at scoring goals and assisting teammates.

A well-liked character off the field, Pelé. He was well-liked and respected by both spectators and his fellow players because of his reputation for good sportsmanship and humanitarian activities. As a worldwide soccer ambassador, Pelé contributed to the sport's globalization. After he stopped playing soccer, he was engaged in some commercial enterprises, such as coaching and team ownership. The legacy of Pelé as one of the best soccer players in history is unquestionable, and he is revered as a real pioneer and symbol of the game. Pelé's passion for soccer was clear throughout his career as he committed himself to it and won countless awards and records. He played soccer at an early age and became quite passionate about it. The passion he had for the game of soccer drove Pelé to work hard, hone his abilities, and support himself throughout his career. Pelé's devotion to soccer indicated how much he loved the game. In addition to representing his nation at the highest levels of international competition, he played professionally for over 20 years. Pelé continued to stay engaged in the sport as a coach, team owner, and television pundit after he finished his playing career. Numerous supporters and other players were inspired by his passion for the game, and future generations will continue to honour him as one of the sport's all-time greats.

It was clear from the manner he played the game. During his playing career, he was seen as the top player in the world due to his talent, speed, and scoring prowess. Pelé was a versatile player who was equally skilled at scoring goals and assisting teammates. He could play as a striker or an offensive midfielder. He was noted for his ability to score amazing goals and was a superb facilitator and finisher. Pelé was renowned for his philanthropic efforts as well as his sportsmanship. He promoted children's rights and heightened awareness of social concerns all around the globe as a UNICEF Goodwill Ambassador. Pelé has participated in some environmental issues, working to save the environment and advance sustainable growth.

Pelé received several honours and prizes due to his passion for soccer and commitment to the game. In addition to being awarded the European Footballer of the Year in 1973, he received three South American Footballer of the Year awards. In addition to being admitted to the Brazilian Football Museum

Hall of Fame and International Football Hall of Fame, Time magazine named Pelé one of the 100 most important persons in the world in 2004. Pele has come under fire for his participation in economic endeavours that have been regarded as questionable or immoral. His participation in a business that generated illicit substances in the 1970s illustrates this. Due to the criticism and outrage that followed, Pele has subsequently expressed regret for his engagement with the business. Political and social opinions held by Pele have also drawn criticism. He received criticism from individuals who supported the Brazilian military dictatorship in the 1970s because he openly backed it. More lately, he has been under fire for his opinions on race and gender, as well as his support of certain nations and politicians. Regarding the charges of sexual misconduct, several women have held Pele accountable for improper actions like unwelcome approaches and sexual assault. Numerous people have criticized and reacted negatively to these claims. The accusations have been refuted by Pele, who asserts that they are untrue. Pele has made several remarks throughout the years that some people have found insulting or provocative. These remarks, which have touched on delicate subjects like race and gender, have often been made in interviews or public appearances.

The movies made about Pele are:

- "Pele: Birth of a Legend" (2018): It tells the story of Pele's early life and rise to fame, including his incredible performance at the 1958 World Cup at 17.

- "Victory" (1981): The biographical drama stars Pele as himself and tells the story of the Brazilian national team's victory at the 1970 World Cup.

- "Pele Forever" (2004): It explores Pele's life and career, including his triumphs on the soccer field and enduring impact on the sport.

- "Pele: The King of Football" (2017): It tells the story of Pele's life and career, including his time with the Brazilian national team and his experiences playing for Santos FC and the New York Cosmos.

- "Pele's Quest for the Cup" (2014): This follows Pele as he travels to Brazil to attend the 2014 World Cup. It includes interviews with Pele and other soccer legends, as well as footage of the tournament.

- "Pele: The Movie" (2016): It tells the story of Pele's life and career, including his time with the Brazilian national team and his experiences playing for Santos FC and the New York Cosmos. It features interviews with Pele and other soccer legends, as well as archival footage of some of Pele's most memorable moments on the soccer field.

Books that Pele has written:

- "Pele: My Life and the Beautiful Game" (2016): The book is an autobiography that tells the story of Pele's life and career, from his childhood in Brazil to his retirement from soccer in 1977.

- "The Beautiful Game: By Pele" (2017): The book is a collection of Pele's thoughts and observations about soccer, including his reflections on the sport's history, its place in culture, and its global appeal.

- "Pele: The Autobiography" (1998): This book is another autobiography by Pele that covers his life and career.

- "Pele: The Master and His Method" (2013): The book is a collaboration between Pele and soccer coach and journalist Harry Harris. It explores Pele's philosophy of soccer and his approach to the game, and it includes insights and advice from Pele on how to improve as a player.

- "Pele: The King of Football" (2013): The book tells the story of Pele's life and career, with illustrations and photographs that help bring the story to life. It is aimed at younger readers and is a great introduction to Pele's life and career for children who are interested in soccer.

CHAPTER TWO

PELE'S PARENT

Soccer player and Coach Joao Ramos do Nascimento was the father of Pelé. In Três Coraçes, Minas Gerais, Brazil, he was born on January 19, 1909. In Três Coraçes, Joao played soccer for some amateur clubs and had a solid reputation as a skilled player. He then became a soccer coach and worked in Brazil with various amateur and professional clubs. Pelé's father also had a prosperous soccer playing career. In Três Coraçes, where he played for several amateur teams, he had a solid playing reputation. Joao was revered and appreciated by his teammates and opponents for his talent, quickness, and scoring prowess.

Pelé was one of Joao's three children from his marriage to Celeste Arantes. Pelé was up in a soccer-centric family and was probably affected by his father's passion for the game. Joao, was crucial to Pelé's growth as a player. He supported Pelé when he started his professional career and encouraged him to follow his love for soccer. Pelé thanked his father for assisting in the growth of his abilities and passion for the game. In an interview with the BBC in 2002, Pelé stated: "My father served as my first coach and instilled in me a love for the game. I owe him so much for all he accomplished for me because of how much I learnt from him." Joao died on October 2, 1972.

Celeste Arantes, Pele's mother, worked as a domestic helper. In Três Coraçes, Minas Gerais, Brazil, she was born on February 21, 1914. Pelé was one of Celeste's three children from her marriage to soccer star and Coach Joao Ramos do Nascimento.

She was certainly instrumental in Pelé's upbringing. She probably gave Pelé love, support, and direction as a mother as he grew up and followed his passion for soccer. Throughout his career, Celeste supported Pelé and was a constant. Pelé praised his mother in a 2002 interview with the BBC, expressing his gratitude for her role in shaping his personality and morals. He said: "I learned so much about life from my mother, who was a really kind and powerful woman. She was always there for me and encouraged me in all I did. She did so much for me, and I am really appreciative." Although Celeste died away on December 10, 2006, her impact on Pelé and his soccer career endures.

CHAPTER THREE

PELE LOVE LIFE

A Brazilian singer and dancer named Rosemeri dos Reis Cholbi was Pele's first wife.

Pele wed Brazilian doctor Assiria Seixas Lemos in his second marriage.

Reis Rosemeri Pele, a well-known Brazilian professional soccer player who was married to Cholbi, a singer and dancer from Brazil, is regarded as one of the game's all-time greats.Pele, wed Rosemeri in 1966. The two had three kids together: Kelly Cristina, Edson Cholbi, and Jennifer. In 1982, Pele and Rosemeri were divorced. And Pele later married to Assiria Seixas Lemos, a physician from Brazil.

Pele had several additional children with other women in addition to those with Rosemeri and Assiria. Marko, Celeste, Edinho, and Ana Cristina are some of these kids.

Pele was renowned for being an engaged parent who actively participated in parenting his children. He has made public remarks on the value of family and urged his kids to follow their goals and hobbies. The children of Pele have succeeded in a variety of endeavors.

The details on each of Pele's children are:

- Kelly Cristina: Kelly, born in 1967, is Pele's eldest kid. She is a singer and television personality from Brazil.

- Edson Cholbi: Edson was born in 1970 and is Pele's second kid. He used to play for many teams in Brazil and Europe as a professional soccer player.

- Jennifer was born in 1975 and is Pele's third kid. She is a model and actress from Brazil.

- Joshua: Born in 1995, Joshua is Pele's fourth kid. He is a soccer player from Brazil who has represented many teams in Brazil and Europe.

- Marko: Born in 1997, Marko is Pele's sixth kid. He is a soccer player from Brazil who has represented many teams in Brazil and Europe.

- Celeste: Celeste was born in 1998 and is Pele's sixth kid.

- Edinho: Born in 2003, Edinho is Pele's eighth kid.

- Ana Cristina: Ana Cristina was born in 2006

- Pele's children have continued in his footsteps and pursued professions in various industries, including acting, music, and sports. Some of Pele's children have also achieved professional success in their own right as soccer players, and they have continued their father's legacy by representing Brazil internationally.

CHAPTER FOUR

HIS SOURCES OF MONEY AND STRUGGLES

Pelé's earnings and financial success may have benefited from his endeavours. He also published a number of books and had popularity as a public speaker, which may have further increased his income. Pelé has taken part in a variety of commercial endeavours. He has been a partner and investor in a number of businesses, including a chain of restaurants and a sports marketing company. He has also participated in charity activities, such as the founding of the Pelé Foundation, which supports several humanitarian initiatives all around the globe.

For his services to soccer and his charitable activities, Pelé has won various honours and distinctions, including the Presidential Medal of Freedom, the Order of Merit, and the Order of the Southern Cross. In honour of his soccer career, he has also received several honours and inductions, including selection by FIFA as one of the "125 Greatest Living Footballers" in 2004 and induction into the Brazilian Football Museum Hall of Fame in 2006.

Despite his many accomplishments on the pitch, Pele's career was not without its struggles. At age 15, he faced numerous challenges throughout his career, including injuries, political upheaval, and financial difficulties.

One of the biggest struggles that Pele faced was dealing with injuries. Throughout his career, he suffered from a number of injuries, including a torn thigh muscle, a fractured ankle, and a dislocated shoulder. These injuries often kept him out of action for extended periods, and he had to work hard to recover and regain his form. Another struggle that Pele faced was the political turmoil in Brazil during the 1960s and 1970s. At the time, Brazil was ruled by a military dictatorship, with frequent protests and unrest. Pele was often caught up in political turmoil, and he faced criticism and backlash for his support of the government.

Pele also struggled with financial issues. Despite his success on the pitch, he was not always well-paid, and he had to deal with contract disputes and financial mismanagement. For example, in the early 1970s, Pele played for the New York Cosmos in the North American Soccer League (NASL). While the NASL was a professional league, it was not as financially stable as other sports leagues, and Pele did not earn as much as he could have if he had played in Europe. Pele's contract with the Cosmos was fraught with legal issues and disputes, and he was often at odds with the team's management over money.Despite these financial struggles, Pele continued to play and perform at a high level. He led the Cosmos to the NASL championship in 1977 and was named the NASL Most Valuable Player in 1976 and 1977. In addition to his success on the pitch, Pele also used his fame and influence to promote the sport of soccer in the United States and worldwide.

Also, Pele was married three times and had several children, but his relationships were often strained, and he experienced a number of breakups and divorces. In addition, Pele struggled with the pressure and demands of being a world-famous athlete, and he often felt overwhelmed by the constant scrutiny and attention from the media and fans. Pele's struggles and challenges only added to his legend and made him a more enduring and memorable figure in soccer. Despite facing numerous setbacks and difficulties, he remained determined and dedicated to his craft. Despite these personal struggles, Pele remained focused on his career and continued to excel on the pitch.

CHAPTER FIVE

PELE'S DEATH

Colon cancer was the reason for Pelé's death. The American Cancer Society estimates that the lifetime chance of having colorectal cancer is 1 in 23 (4.3%) for men and 1 in 25 (4%), respectively. According to the group, in 2022, there will be 106,180 new instances of colon cancer and 44,850 new cases of rectal cancer. According to data from the American Cancer Society, colorectal cancer is the second most prevalent cancer-related that causes death for both men and women in the country and ranks third overall. Additionally, the group states colorectal cancer would be responsible for around 52,580 fatalities in 2022. Audrey Hepburn, Chadwick Boseman, Eartha Kitt, and Kirstie Alley are just a few more famous people that passed away from colon cancer.

Pelé had been forthcoming about his condition before his death. After complications from a fractured rib, he had surgery in 1977 to remove his right kidney. Jose Fornos Rodrigues, Pelé's advisor, told the Associated Press in 2014 after Pelé was hospitalized for a urinary tract infection: "the kidney was removed a long time ago, his body is already adapted to it, it's not an issue at all." Pelé was receiving "temporary" renal therapy at the time, according to Rodrigues, who also said that Pelé was "lucid" and capable of breathing on his own and regularly eating in the critical care unit. Doctors used hemodialysis, a sort of intravenous renal therapy, to remove waste from his blood to help fight the illness. In a statement at the time, Albert Einstein Hospital noted that "the sole (kind of) bacterium found thus far is responsive to the medicines being treated."

An infection developed two weeks after Pelé's second operation to remove kidney stones. After having to postpone an appearance at the Pelé Museum in Santos, Brazil, because of stomach trouble, Pelé was diagnosed with kidney stones. Pelé was discharged from the hospital a few days after the operation due to the procedure's success. The right hip of Pelé had a complete hip arthroplasty procedure in 2012. It was a relatively straightforward procedure, and everything went perfectly. At the time, Rodrigues informed the Associated Press that he would probably depart the next day. In 2016, Pelé had a second hip operation. In addition to having this minor reparatory treatment, "[Pelé] took use of his vacations to spend time in

New York with his children and granddaughters," his press representative Pepito said at the time, according to Reuters.

In the 2018 FIFA World Cup in December 2017, Pelé was seen in a wheelchair. News of Pelé's hospitalization and subsequent breakdown came a month later. According to a Football Writers ' Association statement, Pele fainted early on Thursday morning. He was brought to a hospital in Brazil, where he underwent some tests indicating acute tiredness. While physicians watch his recovery, he continues to drink fluids. Fortunately, there is no indication of anything more severe than fatigue. In 2019, Pelé had another operation to remove kidney stones after being sent to the hospital with another urinary tract infection. Agencia Brasil said, "the treatment was successful, and he is already in the room, in excellent general health from a clinical point of view." Additionally, at the time, Pelé tweeted, "Thank you for all your affection! Both the testing and the antibiotics are effective. I'm ready to resume playing now that I feel so much better!

In a TV Globo interview in February 2020, Pelé's son Edinho, whom he had with Rosemeri dos Reis Cholbi, disclosed that his father could not walk alone. At the time, Edinho said, "He's humiliated; he doesn't go out or be seen or do anything that requires leaving the home." He is quite bashful and secretive. Edinho revealed that Pelé's illness was caused by the fact that he had not completed the physical rehabilitation his physicians had advised after a hip surgery. He is rather delicate. His rehabilitation wasn't sufficient or perfect after his hip surgery, according to Edinho. 'He has a mobility issue, which has led to a mild form of depression. Imagine the monarch is no longer able to walk correctly despite always having such a commanding presence'.

CHAPTER SIX

HOW PELE DIE

At the Albert Einstein Hospital in So Paulo, Brazil, Pelé passed away on December 29, 2022. He was 82 years. Pelé's representative at the time, Joe Fraga, issued a statement that said, "The king has departed." In an Instagram post at the time, Kely Nascimento, Pelé's child with Rosemeri dos Reis Cholbi, also announced her father's death. She posted a picture of herself and several people clutching Pelé's hand, saying, "All that we are is due to you. "We adore you without end.

Pelé passed away one year after having a malignancy on the right side of his colon surgically removed at Albert Einstein Hospital in September 2021. The tumor was discovered during a normal cardiovascular and laboratory examination, according to the hospital. "Dear Friends, I want to express my gratitude for your nice words. I thank God for my good health and for enabling Drs. Fábio and Miguel to look after it," Pelé said in an Instagram post at the time. Last Saturday, I had surgery to remove a suspicious tumor from my right colon. During the exams I described last week, the tumor was found. He kept going, Fortunately, I'm used to joining you in jubilating at significant successes. I shall go into this game with a grin, a lot of hope, and excitement for living amid my family and friends affection. At the time, Pelé was in the critical care unit at Albert Einstein Hospital, but it was anticipated that he would soon be transferred to another room, according to NBC News.

A week had passed since word of Pelé's hospitalization at Albert Einstein when the procedure took place. "Guys, I didn't pass out, and my health is excellent. I took my normal examinations, something I had previously been unable to complete because of the epidemic. At the time, he tweeted, "Let them know I can't play next Sunday. Pelé got a second operation for the tumor in his intestines in December 2021, shortly after which he began chemotherapy at Albert Einstein Hospital. In a statement at the time, the hospital said that the patient was stable and would likely be discharged soon.

In November 2022, eleven months later, ESPN Brazil announced that Pelé had been taken to Albert Einstein Hospital for "general edema," as well as heart problems and worries that his chemotherapy treatment wasn't working as it should. At the time, Kely said via Instagram that "no fresh terrible forecast" had been made. "My dad's health is the subject of a lot of fear in the media today," she said. He is managing medicine while he is in the hospital. Neither a fresh catastrophic forecast nor an emergency exists. I vow to upload pics when I'm there for New Year's. Albert Einstein Hospital said that Pelé had been placed under "elevated care" due to "kidney and cardiac dysfunctions" a month later, in December 2022, and that his cancer had worsened. With all the love and care that this new family at Einstein provides for us, we agreed with the physicians that, for various reasons, it would be best for us to remain here! Kely stated in a post on her Instagram at the time. We appreciate the affection you continue showing for us internationally and locally in Brazil. We feel relief knowing we are not alone, thanks to your love for him, your stories, and your prayers. We wish everyone who celebrates Christmas that is full of family, full of kids, some arguing, and plenty of love and health! After a week, Pelé passed away. Fans paid tribute to Pelé before his passing during the Qatar 2022 FIFA World Cup. "Friends, I'm here at the hospital for my routine checkup. Receiving encouraging notes like these is always welcome. Thank you to everyone who gives me positive energy and to Qatar for this tribute! Early in December 2022, Pelé published a picture on Instagram with a projection of his face reading, "Get well soon," over a Qatari skyscraper. Pelé also advised his fans to keep their cool and think positively in another Instagram post from that period. "I continue my therapy as normal, and I'm strong and full of optimism. I would want to show my gratitude to the whole medical and nursing staff for the treatment I have received," he stated. "I have a strong hope in God, and I am energized by each word of love I get from you throughout the globe. Observe Brazil's World Cup performance as well! I appreciate everything very much.

CHAPTER SEVEN

PELE'S CAUSE OF DEATH AND HOW TO
PREVENT IT

A Cancer called colon cancer affects the colon, often known as the big intestine or large intestines. An organ of the digestive system called the colon is a long, hollow tube-like structure. Through the rectum and anus, it takes in water and nutrients from food, and stores and excretes solid waste. When healthy colonic cells experience DNA alterations, colon cancer starts to spread. These alterations enable the cells to multiply and expand out of control, resulting in a tumor. Without treatment, the tumor has the potential to grow and spread to other body regions. Constipation or diarrhea, stomach discomfort or cramping, rectal bleeding, and weight loss, are all possible symptoms of colon cancer. A colonoscopy is a treatment that enables a doctor to inspect the inside of the colon using a flexible, lighted tube. Colon cancer is often detected by a combination of tests, including this. In addition to surgery to remove the malignant tumor, chemotherapy, radiation therapy, and targeted therapy are all effective treatments for colon cancer. The prognosis for individuals with colon cancer varies in the stage of the disease at the time of diagnosis, the patient's age, and their general health. Early identification and treatment may greatly increase the odds of a favourable result.

Many risk factors may raise a person's likelihood of getting colon cancer. These comprise:

Age: People over 50 have a higher incidence of colon cancer.

Family history: Those with hereditary non-polyposis colorectal cancer (HNPCC) or certain inherited genetic disorders, such as familial adenomatous polyposis (FAP), are at an increased risk of getting the illness.

Personal history: Individuals with a history of colon cancer or precancerous polyps (abnormal growths) that have been removed from the colon are at a higher risk of acquiring the illness.

Diet: A diet heavy on red or processed meats and light on fresh produce and nutritious grains may raise your chance of developing colon cancer.

Inactivity: Colon cancer risk is higher in those who don't exercise regularly.

Obesity: Overweight or obese individuals may have a higher chance of developing colon cancer.

People may take some measures to lower their chance of getting colon cancer, which are:

Get a checkup: Regular colonoscopies or other colon cancer screenings may aid in the early detection of precancerous polyps or cancer when therapy is most successful. The American Cancer Society advises starting colon cancer screenings at age 45 for persons with an average risk of the disease.

Consume a nutritious diet: Red and processed meats should be limited, and fruits, vegetables, and whole grains should be abundant.

Regular exercise may lower your chances of developing colon cancer. Try to exercise for at least 150 minutes a week at a moderate level or 75 minutes at a strenuous intensity.

Maintain a healthy weight: Colon cancer risk may be increased by being overweight or obese.

Avoid smoking: Smoking raises the risk of colon cancer and many other cancers. Quitting smoking may greatly lower your risk if you smoke.

Limit your alcohol intake: Drinking too much might raise your risk of colon cancer. Men should limit their daily alcohol intake to two drinks, while women should limit their daily alcohol intake to one.

Printed in Great Britain
by Amazon

19423277R00020